I0816147

Sue Deagle

Do Loss

A new way to move through change.

For Connor and Kendall

Published by
The Do Book Company 2026
Works in Progress Publishing Ltd
thedobook.co

To find out more about our company, books and authors, please visit **thedobook.co** or follow us **@dobookco**

5 per cent of our proceeds from the sale of this book is given to The DO Lectures to help it achieve its aim of making positive change: thedolectures.com

Cover designed by James Victore
Book designed and set by Ratiotype
Printed and bound in the EU by OZGraf on Munken, an FSC® certified paper
GPSR: productsafety@thedobook.co

The information in this book has been compiled by way of general guidance and is not intended as a substitute for mental health or medical expert assistance. If such assistance is required, the services of a professional should be sought.

A CIP catalogue record for this book is available from the British Library

ISBN 978-1-914168-58-1

10 9 8 7 6 5 4 3 2 1

Contents

Prologue

If you're reading this, chances are you've lost something. Not your keys or your umbrella. Something more.

— A job
— An opportunity
— Your home
— Your health
— A relationship
— A dream
— A loved one
— Yourself

Whatever it is, it's something that leaves a mark. It might have been sudden or long anticipated. Catastrophic, or seemingly small. Yesterday, or quite some time ago.

And what's left is a blank space, hard-to-manage feelings, and the disorienting realization that your life no longer follows the script you thought you were living.

If this sounds like you (or someone you know), read on…

Introduction

A few years back, I had this idea. I wanted to change the conversation around loss.

Because here's what I noticed: we're terrible at this. Whenever we're facing a loss, we avoid discussing it — whether it's ours or someone else's. We hide from loss. We pretend it won't happen to us. Then when it does hit, we're completely unprepared.

We tell ourselves stories that don't help. That loss makes us 'less than'. That we should handle it alone. That talking about loss makes it worse. We've spent our lifetimes learning how to keep our losses hidden, convinced that falling apart means we are weak.

The stories we tell ourselves are doing us no favors. I refuse to accept that any longer. Not for myself. Not for you. Not for any of us.

Because that's not my experience. Nearly ten years after a catastrophic loss turned my world upside down, I live a life that's bigger than I ever imagined.

This book is exactly what the title says: a new way to move through change. Instead of avoiding loss until it forces itself on us, we're going to learn how to navigate it. We'll start with some real talk about what loss actually is and how we typically react. I'll share what I discovered about moving from avoidance to knowledge and navigation, including insights from one group particularly well versed in loss: the military. I'm going to tell you my story and show you the approach I came up with — a mindset shift and a playbook — that works for all kinds of loss. We'll finish by looking at how to get better at this over time, and how to support each other along the way.

Throughout, I'm going to ask you a question or two. Not a worksheet full of tasks, but a pause to check your beliefs, experiences, and understanding. A dip below the surface that helps you question your own ideas on loss. You'll find these as moments to 'Take stock' at the end of sections. Feel free to scribble your responses either on the page or in a notebook.

So, think of this book as a companion on your journey. Dog-ear these pages. Write in the margins. Argue with me when something doesn't fit your experience. Take what helps and leave what doesn't. Because this isn't just a book to read — it's a navigation system to use.

Your journey won't look exactly like mine... or anyone else's. But with each page you turn, you're making a choice: to face your loss with active participation, to grow through what you're going through, and to discover what's still possible on the other side.

Let's begin.

1
Backstory

I had one of those free-range childhoods.

Out the door early, exploring the creeks, fields, and pastures surrounding my rural neighborhood with a gaggle of other kids. We'd ride our bikes to exhaustion, put on plays in the front yard, walk to the community swimming pool for a dip on a hot day. Then back at night for supper with the family.

This was the late 70s and early 80s in western Pennsylvania. Steel country. Blast furnaces burned bright. The mills dotted the rivers — Monongahela, Allegheny, and the Beaver River running through my town: Beaver Falls.

I was focused on typical teenager stuff: swim team, algebra, my first real boyfriend, Dan. Global economics? Not on my radar. But while I was worried about tests and time trials, everything was falling apart around us. Steel mills started closing — first one, then another, then another. Heavy chains went up around the gates where our dads had worked for decades. All that work was shipped overseas. We became another Rust Belt casualty.

After the mills closed, everything else started dying too. Laid off steelworkers weren't taking their families to the Chippewa Hot Dog Shoppe or Sal's Pizza anymore. At first it was just strange that our dads were home during the day. We'd return from school and there they'd be, doing projects around the house, tinkering in the garage.

But then the real consequences set in. Trips were canceled. Expenses trimmed. No more McDonald's after swimming. No more ice cream after church.

Things became more serious. While assuring us everything would be okay, my parents told us we'd have to move. A 'For Sale' sign went up in our front yard. Mom took a job an hour away in Ohio and was gone during the week. I watched my friends' families struggling too. This wasn't how life was supposed to work.

My dad spent his unemployed days retooling. Learning new things. Going for job interviews. Staying calm on the surface. But the clues were all there. I'd sit on my bed with our white fluffy cat in my lap as potential buyers toured the house, deciding if my bedroom was the right size for their kid. Whether the paint color I'd picked out and painted myself when we first moved in suited them. Everything I thought was permanent suddenly wasn't.

After a year of unemployment, my dad got a job.

The buyers of our house agreed to let us out of the deal. I was so relieved. I got to spend the rest of high school in that house. Moving would have been awful and disruptive. It all worked out okay.

That was my first big lesson in loss.

I didn't sail out of that experience with a "whew, dodged that bullet!" attitude. Exactly the opposite.

That experience changed how I saw life: as something filled with uncertainty and insecurity. Life became something I needed to control.

I remember thinking, "No way am I going to let this happen to me again."

So I got focused. I made a plan: only rely on yourself.

First step: university. Second? A good, solid job as a systems engineer, even though I'd never coded a day in my life. But it was the early 90s and anything with computers spelled security. Would I actually like the work? Who cares? I knew I'd like the security of the paycheck and the path it put me on to succeed.

A few years in, I realized I was not going to climb the career ladder at the accelerated rate my anxiety required, so I decided to get a master's degree in business. Because if you're an American capitalist with an MBA, you're absolutely going to be able to provide for yourself forever. Sign me up.

In 1994 I showed up in the steamy heat of Durham, North Carolina — hundreds of miles and a cultural chasm away from steel country — to take my spot in the class of 1996 at Duke University's Business School. Back then, there were 20 per cent women at business school and 80 per cent men. It was like shooting fish in a barrel. On the very first day of orientation, I met a gorgeous blue-eyed boy in the picture-taking line.

My future husband, Mike.

I managed to secure my 'provide for myself' future with both a master's degree and a partner. Then I proceeded to do all the usual corporate things: get a job, then a better one.

One of the things that made Mike and me so well suited was that we had the same tapes running in the background of our brains. Mike was raised by a single mom he adored who constantly worried about making ends meet. He wanted to chase away the monsters of uncertainty too. Sadly not in time to help his mom: she'd died of breast cancer four years before we met.

So that was us: two high-powered careers, building our fortress of control. P&Ls and bottom lines, PowerPoints and strategic plans were our bread and butter, all in the service of career security.

We had two children — Connor and Kendall — and a house we loved. We spent family vacations building elaborate sandcastles on sunny beaches and carving up Rocky Mountain ski slopes. We spent our lives on conference calls and in meetings, clients calling, bosses demanding, kids growing, careers expanding, earnings compounding. We felt stressed but safe.

We were on a roll.

By 2016, we'd built exactly the life we'd planned. Mike traveled during the week for his consulting job. I ran a large team at my defense contracting company. Friday nights were movie nights — pizza and snuggling up with the kids on the couch. Saturday mornings Mike would make pancakes while I went to yoga. They'd be playing cards on the back porch when I got home. Then we'd all head off to lacrosse, track, or swimming, standing around with other parents as the kids did their thing. We had college funds in place, retirement accounts at the ready. We'd gotten so good at this life that we were already talking about where we'd travel when the kids left for college. We'd beaten the system that took down our parents.

And then, one night in November of 2016, I woke up to find my fit, 50-year-old, blueberry-and-kale-eating husband on the floor, unresponsive. I called 911. I performed the CPR I'd learned back in my Pennsylvania lifeguarding days.

The paramedics arrived swiftly and took over, one of them drawing me around the corner so I couldn't see them working on Mike. He asked me questions about Mike's health, his medicines, his meal the night before, writing my responses in a cryptic shorthand on the inside of his forearm with a black ballpoint pen. Like my husband's life could be summarized in a few words scrawled on a stranger's skin.

They rushed Mike off in an ambulance. I called my sister, threw a sweatshirt over my pajamas, grabbed my keys, and raced to the hospital.

When I arrived, a social worker took me to a tiny room with a love seat, a chair, and a coffee table with a box of tissues sitting in the center. Then a downcast doctor entered, sitting down across from me.

"Mrs. Deagle, we could not restart your husband's heart. I'm so very sorry."

Mike was gone.

2
The essential truths of loss

Let's pause for a moment. Let's zoom out and spend some time talking about loss itself. Loss in the general sense, not attached to my life. Not attached to yours.

As I mentioned in the Prologue, there are so many things we can lose. But we don't group them all together and think about 'our losses'. We'd prefer to think they are one-offs, exceptions to the rule. We want to hope like crazy that our last loss will be exactly that — our last loss.

But that's not how this works.

Types of loss

Many of us have experienced a **life-altering loss**, the most 'straightforward' form of loss. A loss that hits us directly and painfully. The loss that may have caused you to pick up this book.

But loss comes in many forms, with different qualities and characteristics. And this is where it can get a little more complicated. Let me explain.

Some losses don't have clear endings. Researcher Pauline Boss calls this **ambiguous loss**. The baby you tried for years to have. The relationship you fought hard to save but still couldn't. The parent whose body is right there across from you, but their mind has gone somewhere you can't reach. These losses leave you hanging. How do you grieve something that was never fully there or never fully gone?

Then there is what I call **anticipated loss**—events you see coming from far away, but they still knock you flat. The empty nest. Retirement. Even the merciful end of a loved one's suffering. You think being prepared will make it easier. Sometimes yes, sometimes no.

Second-hand loss is when you haven't experienced the loss directly but are still deeply affected by it. When your spouse loses their best friend. When a coworker loses their job, while you keep yours. This view from the sidelines can bring on guilt or shame, with questions like "why them and not me?" or "why am I so upset when I'm not directly affected?"

We've all been part of **collective loss**, when our social circles, communities, or nations are impacted by a tragedy. Think 9/11 in New York and DC, Grenfell Tower in London, the Australian wildfires, the global pandemic. Our connections sustain and support us in good times, and we grieve together when loss is shared.

And sometimes loss shows up as the price of something good—these are **bittersweet losses**. You get your dream job but have to move away from your best friend. You finally leave that loveless marriage but miss being part of a couple. These losses come wrapped in relief and guilt all mixed together. I love how Susan Cain frames it in her book *Bittersweet*—we're constantly holding joy and sorrow at the same time. That's not confusion, that's being human.

TAKE STOCK

Which category did your last loss fall into?

How loss behaves

I've spent a lot of time thinking about how loss actually works. Not just from my own experience, but from watching friends, reading books, studying the science, exploring the philosophers, and paying attention to the real-life patterns of loss in everyday living.

Here's what I found:

Loss is inevitable. It's going to happen to you, to me, to every person I've ever met. It's not a matter of *if*, it's a matter of *when*. And it's not just going to happen once.

Loss is cyclical. It has its own rhythm. Sometimes you're in a peaceful stretch, sometimes you're getting hit hard. You're not losing all the time. It ebbs and flows.

Loss is unpredictable. It sneaks up on you. Sure, some losses we see coming from a long way away, but most are unplanned and unexpected. But even when we do expect it, how we actually feel about it can still blindside us.

And here's the odd one: **loss is universal.** I say odd because every single time we lose something, we feel completely alone in that loss. Like we're the only person experiencing it. But actually? We're sharing this common outcome of being human with everyone who's ever lived.

> TAKE STOCK
> **Does this surprise you?**
> **Are there any characteristics of loss you'd add?**

How we react

Here's the thing we're all really hoping to avoid: actually feeling our losses.

I like to call the emotions we're running from 'the Ds'.

Say you had a small loss — disappointment.

Say you had a really big loss — devastation, despair, despondency, damage.

And of course, there are all kinds of other words — words for almost every letter in the alphabet — that we're also trying to avoid: fear, anxiety, uncertainty, anger, fury, embarrassment, regret. You name it, loss invokes it.

When our loss-driven emotions kick in, we stick our fingers in our ears. "Ahh, no, la la la, this is not happening to me! I'm not going to feel this!" Then we jam that alphabet soup of emotions down in the deep, dark recesses of our souls where they can (fingers crossed) fade away over time, unseen.

Or maybe we dump our loss emotions on other people. We take our anger out in a shouting match with our spouse. We take our frustration out on a slow-moving motorist. We take our uncertainty out on our friends, backing out of a long-planned trip.

And there's always the option to avoid others in the hope of avoiding our emotions. One warm hug and heartfelt question — "How are you?" — can send us into uncontrolled crying. So we take to our rooms, leaving phone calls unreturned and plans canceled. We keep those tough emotions to ourselves.

> TAKE STOCK
> **Think about your most recent loss.**
> **How did you react?**

The uniqueness of loss

While we can find some patterns to loss — its behaviors, its emotional effects, its complications — how loss impacts us at the individual level varies. Our life experiences are not the same, so why would we expect our experience of loss to be identical?

The loss of a job at 21—when you're unencumbered, resilient, with decades ahead to rebuild—bears little resemblance to losing your livelihood at 55, with kids to support and a mortgage to pay. The death of a parent in your twenties—perhaps your first intimate encounter with mortality—is different than losing a parent in your sixties after a lifetime with them.

This uniqueness extends to how we handle these losses. What works for you might not work for me. And vice versa. In fact, what worked for you during your last loss might not work as well for your next. That doesn't make our choices right or wrong, it just shows how specific they are to time and place.

Understanding this frees you from all the 'shoulds'—how you should feel, what should help, when you should be 'over it'. There is no standard timeline, no regular prescription. There is only your loss, your context, your way to move through change.

Loss = change

"I just want things to get back to normal."

This universal plea echoes through hospital waiting rooms, law-firm conference rooms, and single seats at the local bar. But loss functions less like a detour (after which we return to our original route) and more like a fork in the road—sending us in a new direction. We have to make way for a new normal.

While our loss is creating a change in our environment—a new family structure, neighborhood, or commute to work—it also creates a change in us. Neurologist Dr. Lisa Shulman taught me something fascinating—loss literally rewires our brains. We form new neural connections in order to compensate for the shake-up, to deal with the change. Our brain is wired to adapt.

So our go-to fear—that loss only makes us less than—is not the entire story. When we navigate it consciously, amid the pain, loss can also bring additional kinds of change. Perspective to our life we couldn't have received any other way. Deeper empathy, clearer priorities, greater appreciation for what remains, and, sometimes, a purpose we never imagined finding.

Not because of some saccharine 'everything happens for a reason' platitude, but because humans possess what researcher Dr. Ann Masten refers to as 'ordinary magic'—our natural ability to adapt. Masten's research shows this isn't some rare gift. It's a capacity we all have that blooms when we have the right support. In her Grawemeyer Awards acceptance speech she said, "Resilience doesn't depend on special qualities but on a capacity to adapt that we develop over time as we are nurtured, learn, and gain experience."

Understanding some of these truths about loss doesn't magically eliminate the pain. Knowledge alone doesn't heal us. But it does provide something essential that can help: context for our experience, language to discuss it, and a foundation for dealing with it.

By zooming out and looking at loss through this lens—from a neutral perspective—we can start to question our beliefs about loss.

TAKE STOCK

Have you been able to return to normal after loss? What, if anything, has changed most for you?

3
Searching for clues

After Mike died, the future was a giant blank space.

Amid that despair and confusion and emptiness, the children — 11-year-old Kendall and 13-year-old Connor — gave me something to focus on. How was I going to make a life for them? How was I going to make sure their lives, their futures, wouldn't be less without a father?

Society might expect less from kids who'd been through this, but I wasn't going to expect less for my own.

I refused to let them down.

A few days after the funeral, we were sitting side by side in a daze on the couch, holding hands. I said, "Listen, things will be different now, but Daddy already built the basement and the first floor of who you are. He's a part of you that way. Yes, we have to finish the second floor without him. But he's already in you. We are going to get through this together."

Now I had to figure out how. As I flailed about in those early days, alternating between all the emotions of loss — despair, numbness, fury, and frustration — three unexpected things changed my trajectory:

— **a conversation**

— **a forest**

— **a realization**

1. The conversation

A different kind of great

Months prior to Mike's death, we'd taken him on a blowout 50th birthday trip to South Africa. We visited the Pretoria Union Buildings, took the Table Mountain Aerial Cableway, and toured the game reserves. We also spent time with our close family friend, and native South African, Wayne. He'd been a presence in our lives since our MBA days.

The day after the funeral, I was sitting alone in my dark living room on one side of the planet while Wayne listened, 8,000 miles away. I described the details of the service, of how so many people had shared their stories of Mike's impact on their life. I listened to Wayne's soothing voice say how unsurprising that was, of course Mike was larger than life in every way.

But then Wayne said something that jolted me:

"Sue, I know it's impossible to see now, but things will be great again."

Oof. Wow. That took a lot of guts for Wayne to say, days into this journey.

But he knew me. He knew the kids. He knew our family. And what he was saying was this: you're not going to reinvent the life you had with Mike. That loss is permanent. That life is over. But there are opportunities for a different kind of 'great' to unfold. Invisible now, but possible down the road.

Wayne's words helped me face the fact that I was not going to get back what I once had, allowing me to mourn instead of railing against its absence. And crucially, they helped me understand that a future I could not see now, could still be bright.

It was the belief in the possibility of what lay ahead. No details, nothing concrete. But something on the horizon: a different kind of great.

2. The forest

Removing the veil of the ordinary

The kids wanted to go back to school as soon as possible. They didn't want to be, as Kendall said, "At home with all these sad grown-ups". They wanted to go where their people were. Where they weren't constantly reminded of their missing father. Where they could be themselves.

My boss gave me six weeks off work, and so, once I got them off to school in the mornings, I had time to myself. Time spent staring at the ceiling in a stupor. Time spent crying on the bathroom floor. Time spent yelling at insurance company representatives. Then the thing I was drawn to the most, the thing that gave me the most peace: time in nature.

I live close by a national park called Great Falls. It contains all the majesty of the Potomac River as it winds around glacier-formed rocks, flowing over churning waterfalls before reaching DC. It's flanked by miles of wooded trails.

Seeking solace, I went every single day.

With my loss-addled brain, I would literally be walking along, numb. But gradually I began taking in the forest in a way I never had before. I'd reach out and pinch a leaf between my fingers. I'd run my palm up the rough bark. I found myself thinking, "How does that leaf feel? How does the tree bark feel?" My brain couldn't really handle much more than that.

Bruce Springsteen describes this phenomenon perfectly in his memoir *Born to Run*. He says that death "removes the veil that the 'ordinary' gently drapes over our eyes".

When loss broke me, I saw my surroundings differently. I saw the details of things I had blindly passed by before. And that's what my brain needed—the veil removed so I could connect with the beauty in the mundane. The everyday. The leaf. The tree. So I could notice things, giving my anxious brain a break.

3. The realization

Letting go of my Lone Ranger approach

Remember that Steel Town strategy? Only rely on yourself. I'd let Mike in, but otherwise I was pretty self-reliant.

But when Mike died, that whole belief system just… crumbled. I didn't even try to fend people off like I usually would.

Help was springing up everywhere around me: my mom cooking meals, my friend Luanne crying with me over breakfast, Connor's teacher Mr. L emailing to recommend Connor skip that day's debate contest.

And for the first time in my adult life, I said yes to all of it.

Maybe it was because my old way of thinking was so completely shattered that I couldn't hold on to those go-it-alone beliefs anymore. Maybe it was because I could see right away that the kids needed more than just me to get by. Maybe it was because I could tell my brain wasn't working properly and I needed some serious backup.

Whatever the reason, I said farewell to my Lone Ranger self. And once I let people in, I discovered something I'd been missing most of my life — I actually needed human connection. Not just wanted it. Needed it.

Those three things changed something for me. Wayne's words gave me something to hold on to. The forest walks gave me peace when nothing else could. Saying yes to help gave me strength I didn't know I needed. I was still deep in grief, still fumbling through most days. But these small discoveries were different from everything else I was trying.

Which got me wondering: what other approaches might be out there? What else might help that I'd never thought to look for? That I'd never been open to finding?

Lessons from unexpected places

When loss hits, most of us haven't the foggiest idea how to navigate. We don't have a map. We don't have a GPS.

We're supposed to figure out a way forward from scratch — stumbling around in the dark, no clue which way is up.

How can we be so unprepared for something that happens to everyone? You'd think we'd have figured this out by now. Surely there are individuals, groups, communities, cultures that have a better understanding of how to deal with loss?

It turns out there is, and one group in particular: the military.

This became clear to me when I took a new job five months after Mike died. This defense contractor role was different from my previous roles in the industry — I traveled to military bases in Europe, the Middle East, the southern US, working alongside servicemen and women and with colleagues who were veterans of Desert Storm and other conflicts. People who had seen loss up close and personal.

One of my colleagues, Karl, a retired Command Chief Master Sergeant in the US Air Force, was open with me from the start about the reality of loss in military life. He treated Mike's death with the deepest respect — listening to me tell stories about him, asking questions, watching out for me on days when he could tell I felt particularly low. We'd take flights together — from Germany to Jordan, from Atlanta to Biloxi, from Kuwait to Qatar — and spend hours talking, bleary-eyed, during late-night layovers in Dubai or early-morning connections in Frankfurt. Karl would let me talk about the kids, about how hard it was to figure out what came next as a single parent. He'd tell me his own stories. He'd share podcasts, videos, ideas that had helped him or others. All the things a friend would do, but with an extra dose of confidence. Never any fear.

Not one of these veterans ever batted an eye when I said I was a widow. Not one. They didn't get that deer-in-headlights look that so many people do. They didn't change the subject or suddenly become uncomfortable. They knew loss was part of life, and they knew how to be with someone who was living it.

But here's what really opened my eyes: they weren't just comfortable around loss — they'd been equipped for it by a massive institution with three centuries of experience, shaped by training that gave them ways to move through it. Not strategies they consciously pulled out but approaches that had become second nature. They use rituals — memorial services, flag presentations, the playing of 'Taps' — for honoring the fallen and creating shared remembrance within a framework rich with tradition. They support each other via a tight-knit culture developed during basic training, far-flung deployments, and shared hardship, enabling them to face loss collectively. Those serving also learn that the mission continues, even when loss occurs, and are given preparation for maintaining operational effectiveness after loss.

Through all these methods, and many more, the military provides predictable frameworks for processing unpredictable losses. It equips our servicemen and women to understand the inevitability of loss — and to face it together.

That's when I realized that these veterans knew something the rest of us don't: the ability to move through loss isn't something you're born with. It's something you can learn.

Looking back, I can see how important this validation was. All that time spent fumbling in the dark, sensing there had to be a better way to move through something so hard. I just didn't know the ins and outs. I didn't know how. Yet.

Karl's military training doesn't exist in normal life. Our broader culture is beyond reluctant to talk about loss. So there are no clear ways to learn how to navigate it.

Think about it: we teach kids how to ride bikes, how to drive cars, how to use technology (scratch that, they teach us how to use technology). But navigate the inevitable losses of life? Good luck with that.

But what if we didn't have to figure it out on our own? What if there was actually a way to learn this?

Looking back, I can see I'd already started collecting clues without realizing it. Wayne's words — "things will be great again" — became part of my vocabulary. I'd repeat them to myself on the hardest days. Bruce Springsteen's line about death removing 'the veil of the ordinary' — I wrote that down on a sticky note and kept it close. Every time I discovered something that helped – forest walks to reset my anxious brain, accepting help instead of going it alone — I doubled down on it. And I took note.

Each clue felt important. Essential, even. Like I was building something, though I couldn't yet see what.

I amped up my search. Broadened my reading to books on loss, memoirs with loss experiences, scientists and researchers describing our brains and bodies under the impact of loss. I expanded the pool of people I spoke with — asking more questions during those airport conversations, paying detailed attention to how different friends moved through their own losses.

What I was building, piece by piece, was my own understanding of how this whole process might actually work. How a conscious, empowered, tool-supported approach to loss might help me move through.

Here's what I kept observing, again and again: there's no magic formula, no one-size-fits-all approach. But there are patterns. Principles that tend to work. Some are about how you think about loss itself, others about specific actions you can take.

And it all starts with what you believe about loss in the first place.

That's where we're going next.

TAKE STOCK

Think about the cultures, groups, organizations in your world: do any of them bring wisdom in navigating loss? Perhaps traditions of your family, church, community group? Where could you search for clues when things go awry?

4 The mindset shift

Most of us are walking around with beliefs about loss we are barely aware of. These beliefs were formed over our lifetimes — consciously or not.

Think about your first big disappointment. Maybe you didn't get into your dream college. Maybe you lost out on a promotion. Maybe someone broke your heart. Those experiences taught you something about how the world works.

Our beliefs are also shaped by watching how our families and friends handled hard times. Did they retreat or move ahead? Did they talk about loss or keep it hidden? Were emotions zinging around everywhere or simmering underneath the surface?

And of course we've also been shaped by our culture. Movies come to mind. There are the straight-up tear-jerkers — *Terms of Endearment* and *Kramer vs. Kramer*. Those laced with humor but still packing a punch — I'm looking at you, *Four Weddings and a Funeral* and *The Full Monty*. Those that show us characters overcoming fear and loss as in *Finding Nemo*, and those that show us personal growth at the end of our trials and tribulations, like *Wild*.

We can't help but take all this information in, run it through our brain's personal filters, and come out with a loss mindset unique to us. Our actions follow: whether we reach out when we're struggling or suffer in silence. Whether we see setbacks as temporary challenges or permanent failures. Whether we think we can grow stronger through difficulty or believe loss only makes us smaller. The problem is most of us never examine these beliefs. We just live by them.

Here are some of the classics I see people, myself included, telling themselves:

— *I should be able to handle this alone* (me all the way)
— *If I don't think about it, it will go away*
— *I need to stay strong for everyone else*
— *I should be over this by now*
— *People will think I'm crazy or weak if I share what I'm thinking about this loss*

The common thread? Don't feel it, don't talk about it. Nothing to see here.

But I was on a different path now. Motivated by the desire to rewrite my kids' futures, the inspiration that the Karls of the world provided, and a slow, hodgepodge gathering of those clues that kept popping up to offer an alternative way to see loss.

I knew the time to question my own outdated, unhelpful beliefs and open my mind to a new way to move through change had arrived.

Because, honestly, I didn't really have a choice.

So I searched. I experimented. I gave things a whirl. I trial-and-errored my way ahead. I discovered some things that didn't work for us: going to the old haunts we'd frequented as a family of four. And a lot of things that did: unlimited ice cream and visits from our fun Uncle Richie, even if it was just to share a pizza and a belly laugh.

I learned. I did more of what worked for us and less of what didn't. And over time, I realized what was getting us through: the belief we'd make it, and the 'doing' that followed. Not flawless, not perfect. We still had epic fails. But we started to have some successes, too.

This process slowly altered my view about what a journey through loss could look like. It rewrote my beliefs from the inside out.

The birth of actionable hope

The change in my beliefs about loss, tested through experimentation, solidified into a new mindset that I now call 'actionable hope'.

Ironic. Because I used to hate the word 'hope'.

Hope seemed like something for people who couldn't take control of their circumstances. People who preferred wishful thinking to actual action. People stuck in place.

But this isn't that kind of hope. This isn't passive waiting or wishful thinking. This is hope that actually does something. Hope with muscle.

The difference matters. Optimism — that cousin of hope that looks the same but isn't — *expects* good things to happen. Actionable hope doesn't wait for good things — it helps *create* them. When you're dealing with loss, it's the conviction that you can take steps to make healing more likely, even when you have no idea what those steps should be.

Actionable hope has three parts:

— openness to possibility
— belief in your capacity to survive and heal
— engaged participation in your way forward

Let me show you what this looked like in my own life.

Openness to possibility

In the early days after Mike's death, my brain would intermittently make predictions: "I'll never be happy again", "the kids are going to live a less-than life", etc. Those predictions felt like stone-cold facts. But then I'd pause. Maybe, just maybe, my brain's disaster scenarios weren't the whole story.

Openness to possibility means catching your brain when it does this fortune-telling thing and saying, "Hold up. That might be true, but I'm not betting my entire future on how I feel right now. I'm not going to give that thought any more power than it deserves. That thought is not the boss of me."

It's not about blind optimism or pretending your loss didn't happen. It's about refusing to let your current situation determine your entire future, even in your own mind.

Belief in your capacity to survive and heal

When loss knocks you sideways, it dents your self-belief. When your doctor sits you down to share a life-altering diagnosis, when your back-of-the-envelope math points to the inevitable loss of your home, when a relationship you relied on disappears... in situations like these, questioning whether you can make it through, whether you have what it takes, is absolutely normal. I'd worry about you more if you *didn't* question yourself, the future, what it's all about. I sure did. In the early days, I definitely had "no way can I do this" moments. But then I'd look at the children. I had to find a way.

Here's what I learned: you don't have to feel strong to be strong. You don't have to feel capable to be capable. The fact that I was still here, making basic dinners and driving people to after-school activities, meant many of my default systems were still in place. And if I added up day after day of doing the default, I could assemble weeks and months that added up to a survival. And, eventually, healing. Putting one foot in front of the other was enough.

We can also get an infusion from resilience researcher Ann Masten here, about our innate ability to survive and thrive. Add in those unspoken lessons that Karl and my military colleagues had been teaching me all along—that survival and healing are the natural outcome after moving through loss—and you can build a belief in yourself. Why would you be the exception to the rule?

Engaged participation in your way forward

This is where actionable hope gets its name. It's not enough to be open to possibility or believe in your capacity. You have to actually do something.

I don't mean you have to have a ten-step master plan or take huge leaps. Remember those daily walks I took at Great Falls? My brain could handle nothing beyond how being there calmed me. Something about the trees, the water, the quiet. So every time I got in the car to drive to the park, I was participating in my own healing rather than just waiting for it to happen to me.

Active participation looked like this: I made myself talk to my far-off friends, Jessica in Minnesota, Julie in Boston, Gillian in Johannesburg. When they called, I picked up. Even when my brain was saying, "Just stare at the ceiling instead—way less effort!" But post-conversation, I always hung up feeling better. Stronger. More hopeful.

Active participation can be that small. It's a fair dose of saying yes when you feel like saying no. Testing whether an action brings you up or drains you. Because sometimes action helps. Sometimes not so much. But choosing to try something, anything, instead of just waiting for time to pass gives you information. You learn what works for you and what doesn't.

One important thing to remember: you need all three elements of actionable hope working together to help you move forward: staying open to possibility, believing in your capacity to heal, and taking action.

It took me time to figure this out. Sometimes I was really good at one area, like staying open to possibility, while feeling completely incapable in others. Sometimes taking even the tiniest action was more than I could muster. But looking back, I could see that when all three did come together, those were the times I felt the most... well, I'll say it: hopeful. Hopeful about the way ahead.

That's what actionable hope gave me — not a constant state of strength, but a mindset I could count on. When I could bring these three elements into my day-to-day thinking, I could feel myself making progress. The measure of that was more good days. Then weeks. Then months. And eventually, years.

> TAKE STOCK
>
> **Which part of actionable hope feels hardest for you — being open to possibility, believing in your capacity to heal, or taking action?**

Building an actionable hope mindset

So how do you build this mindset?

Start with catching yourself. When your brain starts making predictions about your future — "I'll never find another job"; "I'll never get over this divorce"; "I'm too old to start over" — notice it. You don't have to believe different thoughts yet, just catch the fortune-telling in action. As Ice Cube says, "check yourself before you wreck yourself".

Then look for tiny evidence that contradicts the disaster story. Not big dramatic proof, just small stuff. You got through yesterday. You had one decent conversation. You managed to handle that phone call. Your brain will resist this — it's so much easier to spot what's wrong than what's working. But you're training it to notice possibilities too.

Next? Take one small action, even when you don't feel like it. Update your résumé. Reach out to an old friend. Try something you've been putting off. Not because you have to fix everything, but because doing something, anything, reminds you that you have some iota of control.

The key is starting small and being consistent. As neurologist Lisa Shulman taught us, you are literally changing how you think. That's our neuroplasticity at work. It might take longer than expected. You're changing your mind while simultaneously dealing with whatever you lost, so cut yourself some slack. But every time you choose the new pattern over the old one, you're strengthening your ability to move through loss instead of getting stuck in it.

My actionable hope mindset was a way of believing, then thinking, then facing the world and the choices in front of me. Next, I needed some practical tools to help me act. Tools I could apply to the place I was in as I moved through my loss and the different situations I would face.

Next stop? The playbook approach.

5 The playbook approach

"So, what do I do now, and how?"

In our quest for answers after encounters with loss, we'd love to have a time-tested set of guidelines. A list of concrete steps. Clear instructions showing the way. Yet while loss is universal, how we move through it varies dramatically from person to person. Your coping style is different from mine. Your support system varies. The loss you're facing — job, relationship, health, identity — has its own unique challenges.

After my mindset shift to actionable hope, what helped me get tactical wasn't a rigid set of steps. It was amassing all my clues and building a Playbook. Over time this became my 'how'.

The concept of a playbook — most familiar from the worlds of business and sport — works remarkably well for navigating loss. Not as a script to follow, but a flexible collection of tactics, techniques, methods, and strategies you can consider and apply during the different phases of your loss.

Think about how coaches use playbooks. They don't script every single move. Instead, they develop sets of plays the team can draw from depending on what's happening on the field. Weather. Injuries. Opponent strengths and weaknesses. Player meltdowns. These all call for adjustments: for choosing a different play that suits the circumstances.

The defense shifts? Your best player gets injured? You are trailing and in danger of getting crushed? You adjust. It's about taking in all the clues, reading what's happening in the moment, and pivoting from there.

I began picking up potential loss approaches – 'plays', if you will — the same way I figured out actionable hope: by paying attention to what actually worked. Not just for me, but from the stories I collected along the way. Conversations with friends. Memoirs written by strangers. People I'd meet who'd shared their own experiences with loss. As I gathered approaches from these different sources, I made mental notes of what made sense to me.

Some were immediate additions to my collection, like when a friend described a ritual that helped her move on from her lost job — sitting side by side at the library with her sister-in-law every Monday while they updated their LinkedIn profiles and polished their résumés. That togetherness during challenging times felt right to me. I could adapt that to my situation too. Other times I thought, "I can't believe they did that! That's something I am definitely not going to try."

Over time, I assembled these trials, experiments, and discoveries into my own personal Playbook — a collection of approaches I could selectively draw from, add to, and refine as I navigated my path forward. Along the way, I incorporated insights from science and psychology to strengthen my understanding. My hope is that what I am about to share with you will help you to navigate your way through the different phases of loss.

The Playbook

My own experience of loss had revealed three phases that I call: **Cocoon**, **Adapt**, and **Emerge**. In the Playbook, I provide specific strategies for each. You can begin with the phase that best matches where you are right now, rather than feeling you have to start at the top if you're already further along. And not all losses have all the phases. Context is everything. You be the judge.

Some of these strategies you'll embrace immediately. Others you'll customize to fit your circumstances. Some you'll dismiss entirely. That's exactly how a playbook should work. Its power isn't in following it precisely. It's in the permission it gives you to choose what serves you, when it serves you, and how it serves you.

Let's start with the first phase: Cocoon.

Cocoon

How you know you're here: It's early days, and you're still processing that this loss is real. You move erratically from one emotion to another. Time feels strange — some moments drag on forever, others disappear completely. Simple decisions feel exceptionally hard. The basics of life are challenging.

This is the phase where you need to pull back and focus on yourself. Just like if you broke your leg — you wouldn't expect yourself to run a marathon. You'd rest, limit activity, focus on healing. Loss requires the same kind of withdrawal. The clichéd journey of a butterfly gives us the visual here: this is the phase of caterpillar soup. The protected space where the messy, necessary work can happen.

This retreat is essential in the intense early period when the loss hits hardest. Those first hours, days, weeks, months when you're still processing that your new reality is indeed your new reality. Pulling back limits distractions and provides the focus you need in these early days of moving through change when everything feels different.

Whether you're dealing with death, divorce, job loss, health changes, or any other major transition, here are six plays that can help you navigate the Cocoon phase:

1. Respect your emotions

Invite these unwanted guests to the party

I spent 48 years avoiding unwanted emotions at all costs. I wouldn't even listen to sad songs on the radio. Then Mike's death obliterated my defenses. Thank goodness.

Without processing emotions, there is no moving ahead.

When loss kicks tough emotions into high gear — anger, anxiety, despair, fear — our brains rebel. This isn't weakness or failure on our part. Neuroscientist Lisa Feldman Barrett explains that our brains are wired to predict and prepare for what might happen next, and when loss disrupts our world, our prediction systems go into overdrive trying to make sense of the threat. We try to run from both the loss and the overwhelming feelings that come with it. But working with our emotions, not against them, is the foundation for healing.

So resist locking your emotions away. Filled with rage? Consumed by anxiety? Feeling hopeless? While this feels like chaos, it's also a healthy dose of information. Facts that help you protect yourself, ask for support, or honor what you've been through.

This means letting yourself cry when you need to cry. Feeling angry without immediately trying to talk yourself out of it. Sitting with sadness instead of rushing to distraction. Punching a pillow. Walking it out. Jumping in the swimming pool and screaming underwater (been there, done that).

Your emotions aren't problems to solve — they're responses to process. Denying them only separates us from ourselves.

> TAKE STOCK
> **Reflect on the emotions that come up for you first after your losses.**

2. Brace for the chaos

Riding the rollercoaster when you didn't buy a ticket

A few months after Mike died, a therapist handed me a piece of paper. It showed an expanded 'stages of grief' diagram shaped like a 'U': denial, anger, bargaining, depression, acceptance, plus a smorgasbord of other in-between stages — fear, shock, numbness — for extra effect. The message: you go down into the depths then recover in a neat, orderly progression. But then she showed an identical drawing with an overlay: spaghetti-style squiggly lines all over the place, zigzagging everywhere, looping back, jumping ahead, creating a complete mess.

"This", she said, "is what any major loss really looks like."

It was exactly how I felt.

My emotions were everywhere — furious one minute, numb the next, then hit with a wave of unexpected gratitude, followed by crushing despair. Then a little awe sneaking in while touching that unfurling spring leaf.

When you're processing a loss of any size, there's no order to it, no tidy progression from one emotion to the next. Loss researchers Margaret Stroebe and Henk Schut have found that we naturally 'oscillate'. You can think of that like the pendulum on a clock — swinging back and forth between feeling the chaotic emotion of the moment, then taking much-needed breaks from them. That's not a sign you're doing it wrong. That's just how it works.

3. Avoid self-judgment

Put your own weapon down

The Buddhists say that any time we suffer a loss, two arrows fly our way. That first excruciating arrow comes from a bow we don't know, i.e. the loss itself. The second arrow? Look down at the vibrating bow in your own hands.

Second arrows sound like:

— *My loss isn't as bad as other people's*
— *Everyone else would handle this loss better than me*
— *I deserved this*
— *I should be strong enough to do this alone*

Whether you're beating yourself up about a lost deal, a job loss, or a health diagnosis you might have caught earlier, these thoughts just add to the stress. When these thoughts arise, picture yourself cocking that bow to shoot yourself. Then put your weapon down.

Try catching yourself: "There I go again, shooting myself with my own arrows."

Sometimes just noticing the pattern is enough to break it. Other times, ask yourself: "Would I say this to a friend going through the same thing?" The answer is a resounding no.

This isn't about denying your assessments but recognizing how we irrationally twist what's happening. Choose what thoughts deserve your attention, and what you'll leave behind.

TAKE STOCK

Do you have a favorite way to beat yourself up for your reactions to loss?

4. Put yourself first

It's time to be selfish

Selfishness gets a bad rap. In the Cocoon phase, you can't be too selfish. Focusing on ourselves feels difficult, like it's not aligned with our values or how we've been raised. But being the center of your own universe isn't just allowed—it's required. These aren't normal times.

If you are not self-centered, there will be no self left to center.

Sometimes it's easier to identify what you don't need—things that set you back, drain your energy, make you feel worse—than what you do. Whether that's avoiding certain people, skipping social obligations, or saying no to requests that feel overwhelming.

Chimamanda Ngozi Adichie gives us courage to focus on ourselves in her slim volume *Notes on Grief*: "I talk only to my closest family. It's instinctive, my recoiling." Her words give us permission to do the same as she teaches us that this desire is a common one.

When people offered me meals, I'd ask them to leave food on the front porch. If I had just calmed myself down from thinking about my messed-up life, I didn't want to relive it with the lasagna-bearing neighbor showing up at the door. If I felt up for a hug, I'd make a surgical dash outside. Otherwise, I'd text a heartfelt thanks.

Rude? If I hadn't just experienced a loss, maybe. But since I had? Rude wasn't a consideration. Survival was.

Most of us don't have much control over the demands on our time and energy. People who rely on us to care for them, jobs we must attend to. This makes prioritizing ourselves a very real challenge. But carve out what time you can, ask for help when you must, limit the draining of your energy to what's strictly necessary.

Having good boundaries and taking care of yourself conserves energy when you have none to spare. Step back. Recharge. Create the space to replenish yourself.

> TAKE STOCK
> **Taking a clear look at your constraints, what are a few realistic ways you can put yourself first?**

5. Cope dirty

If it feels good, do it

We think there must be appropriate and inappropriate ways to cope. Surely it's not a free-for-all?

But actually, it is.

We judge how others handle losses: "I'd never do that." The truth? You have no idea what coping mechanisms you'd reach for in their shoes.

My guidance for coping in the Cocoon phase is simple:

Whatever works.

Resilience researcher Dr. George Bonanno defines coping as "whatever gets you to the end of this moment". My own version? *Star Wars* movies on repeat.

The kids would come downstairs and find me, glassy-eyed and zoned out, watching Han Solo and Princess Leia for the gazillionth time. They'd take one look at my vacant stare and quietly give me space. They understood, even without words, that I needed a mental break.

We assume coping must be productive, edifying, or virtuous. That it must advance our healing. What we fail to understand is that sometimes, the Millennium Falcon and mental checkout are exactly that.

Free yourself. Embrace the seemingly inconsequential things that help you survive. You might reach for wine, comfort food or trashy TV. Tuning into what you need right now builds a lifelong skill for navigating not just loss, but life itself.

> TAKE STOCK
> **What are your *Star Wars*-type coping strategies?**

6. Accept support

Even the Lone Ranger had Tonto

We have a thousand creative ways to talk ourselves out of accepting help. Our excuses sound like:

— *My loss is too small. Others need help more.*
— *My loss is too big. I don't want to burden anyone.*
— *My loss is too embarrassing. I'll be judged.*
— *What if my people don't come through? That would hurt even more.*

But in my experience? Our loved ones want to support us. They want to make a difference. Instead of pushing away support, try seeing it differently. You're running on empty. Your helpers have energy to spare. Let them help recharge you.

In the early weeks of my loss, my friend Denise flew in from Boston to do my Christmas shopping. She cooked meals every night and sat by my side as I opened that day's batch of sympathy cards. She didn't try to fix my sadness — she just handled the logistics I couldn't manage. Her calm presence recharged me enough to face the next day.

Another friend Takis was attuned to the mundane aspects of my day-to-day life and what might go sideways to make an already bad time worse. He filled my slow-leaking car tire before it became a full-fledged flat. He scanned my insurance forms before I submitted them. He helped me understand my finances when my brain couldn't add or subtract. His kind actions meant I didn't face a nasty surprise I was too exhausted to anticipate.

Then there's the emotional backup. When I couldn't bear taking my daughter to the just-released Disney movie (ever notice the unrelenting loss in Disney movies?), my brother-in-law Richie stepped in and delighted my daughter with giant popcorn and the patience to stay through the end credits. Bonus: he delivered a happy girl back home while I had two hours for a quiet walk.

Support often comes when you least expect it. My daughter's schoolmates made her sympathy cards, giving her a tangible way to feel looked after. Night after very dark night, she read and re-read them. My son's teacher did regular check-ins, guiding me on what activities he observed energized Connor (basketball) and what were too much of a strain (debate team).

Together, these small acts became the support structure that held me up. When we stop pushing help away, we discover we're not as alone as we thought.

> TAKE STOCK
>
> **Who are three people who you know will step in to support you?**

As we wrap up this Cocoon phase, something shifts. We're not more put-together. We're more human. Fragile, raw, humbled. Yet somehow more connected to our humanity, more compassionate toward our mood swings, more certain that we weren't built to go it alone.

Then one day you'll experience an unfamiliar emotion: a burst of feeling like... yourself. That's when you'll know you're ready for the next phase.

Adapt

How you know you're here: Reality has settled in. You start to look outward again and find yourself open to doing things. Sometimes it's smooth, sometimes it's a little off-balance and awkward. Anxiety and curiosity share your brain space. Others may nudge you with a message: "It's time to move on." At times, you'll even agree. But how?

While the Cocoon phase was about purposeful retreat, the Adapt phase is about shifting from reacting to taking the initiative. It's about re-entering your altered life. This is where you start taking actions—thoughtfully and on your own terms—and build mini success stories through the completion of tasks, successful interactions, or just the marking of a ho-hum day where the thought of your loss did not dominate. It's anchored around figuring out the things that consistently help you feel more like yourself again, then experimenting with adjusting those inputs. Much of the adapt phase is adapting to yourself. Your loss has changed you, and you need to get comfortable in your new skin.

Here are five plays to help you navigate through the Adapt phase as you shift from defense to offense.

1. Find your personal regulators

Download your nervous system's favorite playlist

When we're navigating loss, we often hear advice about what we 'should' do to feel better. Exercise more. Connect with friends. Practice gratitude. While these suggestions come from a good place, they miss something crucial: what helps bring one person back to equilibrium might completely overwhelm you.

Neuroscientists call this coming back into balance 'regulation'. It might sound a bit official but, I promise, no permits are required. Just an awareness on your part of the activities and inputs that bring you back to steadiness. The 'doing' and 'receiving' of personal regulation.

As you move into this Adapt phase, identifying and adjusting your personal regulators is the task at hand.

To be clear, I don't mean the universal things we all need—love, safety, purpose, food, and shelter. We aren't doing Maslow's hierarchy of needs here. I mean the specific elements that help you regain your footing. The things that consistently help you feel more like yourself.

I see this with my own kids: one thrives on spontaneity and last-minute adventures, while the other needs routine and predictable structure to feel secure. What energizes one would drive the other around the bend. The same is true for all of us. Your sibling might recharge through physical activity while you recharge through creativity. Your partner might need variety and stimulation while you find peace in quiet, repetitive tasks.

So how do we do this?

Ask yourself a few questions. What lights you up? What shuts you down? I like to go back to what gave me peace or positive energy as a kid and look there for clues.

Loss or no loss, we're drawn to activities, people, practices that expand us. And we have a pretty good feeling about what contracts us, too. Psychologist Kristin Neff's research on self-compassion backs this up; we often know what we need more than we give ourselves credit for. Listening to ourselves — instead of following conventional wisdom or others opinions — is where the rubber meets the road.

In my personal search for what made me feel better, I began to see patterns. I saw that walks in the woods gave me peace. My Saturday reading ritual of the *Financial Times Weekend* was not just an activity to keep my corporate mind on task, it also occupied my brain and helped me discover cool and quirky new things.

I also observed that being in too-crowded conference rooms, attending fancy galas, and dealing with difficult clients stressed me out or sent me into a tailspin.

Of course, some things were not choices — difficult clients are difficult clients and part of the job — but after an interaction that had gone south, I could still feel myself slide.

Through all this back and forth, I looked for the commonality in what gave me the best feel-good reactions, whether that was peacefulness, joy, contentment, stress release, or distraction. Over time I came up with my own list of regulators:

- **Connection:** time with friends, family, supportive strangers
- **Solitude:** alone time to regroup, recharge, read
- **Nature:** walks in the woods, time by water
- **Movement:** hiking, running, swimming
- **Curiosity:** ideas, inspiration, distraction
- **Rest:** sleep, meditation, staring at the ceiling

Looking back at my list, some might seem contradictory—how can I need both connection and solitude? But that's exactly the point. Some days I needed deep conversation with a close friend. Other days I needed to disappear into the woods alone with my thoughts. Both are essential to who I am, just at different times and in different doses.

Your list will not look like mine. You may have birdwatching or going to the gym, cooking or gardening, gaming or live music. Maybe you need art, organized spaces, working with your hands. This part of the Playbook is a search for what suits you, custom-made to your needs. The key is identifying what consistently brings you back to yourself.

> TAKE STOCK
> **What are five things you do that consistently affect how you feel?**

2. Adjust your regulators

Dial it up, dial it down

Once you know your personal regulators, the next step is learning how and when to adjust them.

To make this concrete, let's picture a rock concert. Now imagine the sound engineer sitting in front of a vast mixing desk with a set of sliders under their fingertips. The sliders control the level of inputs—vocals, drums, guitar, bass—and the engineer adjusts the levels to create the best sound. They don't set everything to maximum volume—that would be chaos. Instead, they constantly adjust the levels based on what the music needs *in that moment*.

During the Adapt phase, this principle of managing your inputs takes practice. But it's at the very core of feeling like yourself again, giving you a strong foundation to move through change.

Let's use my regulators to think this through. Maybe I slide *Rest* way up because I'm emotionally and physically exhausted. I might turn *Movement* to medium because gentle walks help, but intense exercise feels like too much right now. And I might slide *Curiosity* almost to zero because learning new things feels overwhelming on days when I am just trying to get by.

You'll adjust your regulators in the same way. The beauty of this approach is that you're not passive in your healing. You're not just hoping you'll feel better eventually. You're actively adjusting what you bring into your life based on what you need right now. And as you move through change, you can tweak those sliders accordingly.

Learning to adjust them is learning to regulate yourself back toward stability with intention. So how do you actually move those sliders? That's where your tools come in. Tools are the specific ways you get more of each regulator.

Here's an example. I already knew how critical being in nature was for me, so having *Nature* on my regulator list was a no-brainer. But where and how would I get my nature fix? And at what dose?

Here were some options:

- **Walking** in the forest and watching for wildlife
- **Listening** to David Attenborough's soothing voice while iguanas danced on my TV screen
- **Watering** (and sometimes talking to) my houseplants

Those tools could all, more or less, get me a version of my nature fix. But if I was traveling for work, I didn't have access to my forest. So it was Sir David all the way. Sometimes you optimize. Sometimes you take what you can get.

But hold on, what if I wasn't sure what I needed? Which of my six regulators was going to do the trick? How could I figure it out?

This brought me to experimenting.

At first, I fumbled around a bit. Some days I'd lean on *Nature*, find myself crying in the forest, then come home lonelier than when I started. But wait, nature was one of my regulators! But it turned out what I really needed was a long conversation with a friend (*Connection!*). I just wasn't skilled enough — yet — to know.

Other days, the forest was just what I needed. The sight of speckled fawns hanging close to their mothers. The woodpecker's rat-a-tat-tat. All of these things brought the beauty of nature into my life when beauty outside of it was in short supply.

That's why it's not a single slider — it's a control panel with multiple options for building the strength we need to put ourselves back together.

This phase is all about tweaking and adjusting based on what's working. This means embracing experimentation — with its inherent letting go of preconceived notions and creating feedback loops to evaluate results.

> TAKE STOCK
> **Pick one of your favorite regulators.**
> **How can you get more of it into your life?**

Here's one more superpower idea when it comes to our regulators: look for combo effects.

When I walked in the woods with the kids, I ticked *Nature*, *Movement*, and *Connection*. The times alone with my newspaper? *Solitude* and *Curiosity*.

Adapting becomes far easier when we experiment to know what lights us up and what pulls the plug. Without it, we might mindlessly repeat tactics that don't work. We might beat ourselves up when things don't go right, or worse, stop trying altogether. Hold up. Cut yourself some slack.

You are building self-trust here. Building this skill becomes invaluable for whatever comes next. You're not just surviving this loss, you're developing a lifelong capability for navigating change.

Your control panel gives you the foundation for navigating the Adapt phase. From here, I've laid out a few additional tools and tactics that I found helpful. Pick what resonates with you and ignore the rest — this is your Playbook to customize.

3. Seek inspiration

Sometimes we lose the plot

A year after Mike died, I found myself in a reading rut. The grief memoirs that had sustained me weren't hitting the same way anymore. I needed something different.

So I gave another genre a try: rockstar memoirs.

I watched Bruce Springsteen process the imminent loss of E Street Band saxophonist Clarence Clemons, attending to him in his hospital room and playing music at his bedside in his final hours. I was surprised by Dave Grohl describing how a month before bandmate Kurt Cobain died, he'd been told Cobain had overdosed in Rome, and had gone through a grieving process then, only to find it wasn't true. Then, when it was real this time, he had to go through that painful spiral all over again.

These memoirs were not offering advice. They were offering an example of the human experience, dressed up in leather and sporting a guitar, but profoundly human just the same. Springsteen and Grohl, plus a shelfful of others, were working through their Adapt phases on the page, in gritty technicolor detail.

Yes, they are famous people. But that wasn't the point. The fact that they were human was. I could relate to their messy processes and mistakes. I could relate to their losses and they inspired me with their blunt talk.

Sometimes the person who shows you what's possible is your neighbor Harry who went back to school to retrain at age 40, or a colleague who moved to a place they always wanted to live after their divorce. Keep your eyes open for examples of people navigating change in ways that spark something in you.

TAKE STOCK

Who have you observed navigating loss? Think broadly here — a movie star, a colleague, or a historical figure? What do you take away from their story?

4. Accept the awkwardness

Of course it feels strange

The first time I went to a work social alone, everyone seemed to be moving faster than me and conversations felt too loud. When colleagues asked, "How are you?" I had no idea what to say. I ended up tucked in the corner by the chocolate fountain chatting with the caterer — someone who didn't know my story. Phew.

This wasn't because I was doing anything wrong. I was relearning how to navigate the world, when everything felt off.

Expect the weird feeling. Re-entering your old world after any major loss is inherently awkward. You're not the same person who left, but everyone else has stayed roughly the same. That's why it's wise to give yourself time to recalibrate. What used to feel natural now requires conscious effort. You need time to adjust to different environments.

And please remember: this is temporary. You're building new skills for navigating the world as this version of yourself. Each time gets a little easier.

> TAKE STOCK
> **Recall an awkward post-loss moment. How did you react?**

5. Trust you are making progress

Even when the scoreboard doesn't show it

By now, chaotic emotions no longer surprise you. Those waves of sadness, frustration, anger still come, but you've learned to ride them rather than being pulled under. Trust those skills. Notice the small signs of progress, even on hard days. The fact that you can recognize your own patterns is itself a testament to how far you've come.

Healing doesn't follow a straight line or a stopwatch, but that doesn't mean you aren't moving forward. Progress happens beneath the surface — you're developing new skills, building resilience, and finding your way through unfamiliar terrain. The scoreboard might not show it yet, but every play you run, every step you take, adds to your strength and resilience.

As you master these adaptations and build confidence in your ability to navigate this changed landscape, you'll start to sense something new stirring. You're not just surviving anymore, or even just adapting. You're beginning to emerge

—discovering who you're becoming and what you want to create from here.

Let's go to the last phase: Emerge.

Emerge

How you know you're here: You feel like yourself again ... but an altered version. A you, 2.0. Emotions still bleed through. Now you know they are just part of being human. And part of being alive.

The Emerge phase is about incorporating your loss into your life and moving forward. Whether from the end of a relationship or a career, emerging isn't about returning to who you were. It's about discovering who you've become because of what you've experienced. And learned.

Here are seven plays for the Emerge phase.

1. Embrace transformation

It's your Cinderella moment

Not every transformation makes headlines. Sometimes it happens quietly, in subtle shifts that only you can feel. Your priorities have changed. Your vision has shifted. You have a different view of what's really important.

I see this most clearly when things go sideways for me or the kids. A minor mishap, a lost wallet, an unkind word from a challenging coworker. Those things used to drain me. Now? I can't say I enjoy the trials and tribulations, but they are small compared to what we've been through. "Nobody died," is how we respond.

Psychologist Dan McAdams has found that major challenges literally make us rewrite our life story—incorporating new values, strengths, and perspectives.

It's time for you to recognize what's different so you can rewrite your story.

Some people keep on expecting the 'old you' to return. Let them know that particular Elvis has left the building. You don't have to be too specific. "I've learned some things about myself" or "My priorities have shifted" will do, just enough to give others permission to adjust their expectations of you too.

2. Claim your strength

Check out your before and after photos

There is nothing more empowering than surviving what once seemed insurmountable. Embrace that strength. The hurt doesn't vanish, but you develop a different relationship with it. You become more confident, more capable of dealing with whatever happens next.

Psychologists Richard Tedeschi and Lawrence Calhoun call this 'post-traumatic growth'. In their article *The Many Layers of Post Traumatic Growth* (Brainline.org), they describe it as "the experience of positive change resulting from the struggle with major life crises. The concept is, of course, ancient and has been prevalent in the literature, philosophy, and religion of almost all cultures."

Their research shows that people often develop genuine new capabilities: stronger relationships, deeper appreciation for life, increased personal strength. "They are open to new opportunities... possibilities and choice that may not have presented themselves before the tragedy."

You've built resilience through countless moments of choosing to move forward when retreating seemed safer. Remember that first time you went somewhere alone after your divorce? When you finally updated your résumé after getting laid off? Each step built your strength.

You've also learned to use your regulators—to read your own signals and respond accordingly. You know what helps you feel better and what makes things worse. You can assess what you need and take action to get it.

Here's another thing you've built: the ability to recognize early-warning signs of emotional struggle and act before you're in crisis mode. No more waiting until you're drowning to reach for help.

Self-knowledge becomes the foundation for navigating transitions and embracing life's uncertainties. You now have a better understanding of what works specifically for you. That's so powerful!

> TAKE STOCK
>
> **What are the skills you've developed, the boundaries you've learned to set, the difficult conversations you can now handle? Collect the evidence.**

3. Let new things fill the vacuum

Loss-shaped holes linger; surprising things fill them

Things won't go back to the way they were. That reality remains. But possibility exists too. You're not looking for substitutes. You're finding new things that fit who you are now.

What new interests, relationships, or practices might fill the spaces in your life? Not as replacements for what was lost, but as additions to a life that continues to evolve. My work friend Ken—more a brother than a colleague to me—would always deliver my favorite sparkling water to my seat at every board meeting, leadership gathering, or dinner outing. He never even knew Mike, but with this gesture, he was looking after me. Filling some of my Mike-shaped hole with his thoughtfulness.

Stay open to surprises while you're on the hunt. Maybe after your divorce you discover you prefer quiet evenings over busy social calendars. Maybe losing your job leads you to interests you never had time to explore. Maybe moving away from family helps you build deeper relationships with neighbors.

You'll also want to experiment deliberately. Try one new thing—a class, a hobby, a different route to work. Notice what sparks curiosity. Pay attention to activities that make you lose track of time.

Then let evolution happen. What fills the gaps might look nothing like what you lost. That's not failure—that's evidence your life is continuing to unfold in ways you couldn't have predicted.

The spaces left by loss don't have to stay empty. But what fills them is entirely up to you.

> TAKE STOCK
>
> **What new interests or relationships might fill the spaces in your life?**

4. Practice integration

Honor what was, while embracing what is

Integration isn't about tucking your loss away, never to be heard from again. Veterans surely don't do that. In the US, our Arlington National Cemetery—a sacred burial ground for fallen service members and their spouses—is a place of national remembrance. A way to keep the lives lost at the forefront of our nation's story. On a personal level, integration's function is about letting your loss become part of your life's story.

You'll know integration is happening when your loss can come up in conversation without derailing your entire day.

When memories can exist alongside new experiences without knocking you sideways.

You might find yourself creating new rituals. I make a small, secretive nod to every red cardinal (our handsome Virginia state bird) I see — whether they are swooping through my back yard in pairs or shaped into a crystal figurine on the gift-shop shelf — as they are a symbol of Mike to me.

The kids and I have also taken our Friday night movie nights and morphed them into lazy Saturdays watching sports. Just different enough to give us together time without always feeling Mike is missing.

The ways loss has shaped you and the adjustments you've made aren't consolation prizes. They're proof that you can handle hard things and come out different on the other side.

5. The binary nature of truth

The dynamic duo of both/and

One of the most liberating discoveries of the Emerge phase is learning that you don't have to choose between contradictory feelings. You can hold more than one simultaneously without it meaning you're confused or failing at recovery.

You're transformed and you're still you. You honor what was lost and embrace what's new. You can feel joy and still have moments of sadness. You've grown stronger and the hurt doesn't vanish.

This isn't emotional confusion — it's emotional maturity.

For years after my loss, I thought I had to pick a lane. Either I was grieving or I was moving forward. Either I missed my old life or I was building a new one. Either I was sad about what I'd lost or grateful for what remained.

The truth was always both.

Stop forcing yourself to choose. Our culture loves clear categories, but loss doesn't work that way. You can miss your ex-husband and feel relieved the fighting is over. You can grieve your lost job and be happy to be away from a difficult boss. You can love your grown-up children and treasure your newfound freedom.

Let duality exist. When you try to force yourself into one emotional box, you end up feeling like a fraud. "I shouldn't be sad when I have so much to be grateful for", "I shouldn't miss that toxic job", "I shouldn't feel lonely when I chose this change". But humans are complex. Our responses to loss are complex too.

This both/and thinking becomes crucial as you navigate future changes. It's what allows you to honor your past while stepping confidently into whatever comes next.

> TAKE STOCK
>
> **Practice using 'both/and'. The next time you catch yourself thinking "I should feel X instead of Y", try "I feel both X and Y". Notice how much more honest that feels.**

6. Let yourself outgrow things

What got you here won't get you there

You may need to let go of certain coping mechanisms, relationships, or habits that were once helpful but now limit your growth.

Three years into my loss, I gradually stopped reading books about death. Those books served me well when I needed them. But my curiosity had shifted—I found myself drawn to philosophy, history, travel books, even fiction. I wanted to focus more on living. I wasn't abandoning my sadness. I was acknowledging my changing relationship with it.

You'll start noticing what's no longer serving you. Maybe that support group that was essential in year one feels draining in year three. Maybe the friend who was perfect for processing grief isn't the right person for celebrating new adventures.

Just because something helped you survive in the Cocoon phase, it doesn't mean you're obligated to keep it forever. What you need changes as you change.

This isn't betrayal—it's growth. You're not rejecting what helped you heal. You're choosing what helps you thrive.

7. Allow yourself to feel joy

Happiness isn't betrayal

Perhaps the most challenging part of emergence is embracing joy without guilt. There's a persistent myth that regaining happiness somehow dishonors what was lost, as if your capacity for joy should be permanently diminished.

Musician Nick Cave, after losing his teenage son, wrote about this beautifully: "Joy is not happiness. Joy is what happens to us when we allow ourselves to recognize how good things really are."

He discovered that joy after loss isn't betrayal—it's often more profound because you understand its preciousness.

There will be times when you feel bad about feeling better. Once at a lunch with my pal CeCe, she cracked a joke that made me laugh out loud. I stopped abruptly. Wait, shouldn't I still be sad? But I paused and said, "I feel like myself again." She said, "I can tell."

The first time you laugh without thinking about your loss, you might feel surprised. That's normal. You're allowed to be happy.

Small moments will sneak up on you: when you realize you've gone a whole day without thinking about what happened; when you feel excited about weekend plans; when something makes you genuinely smile. Let yourself feel these fully without immediately thinking about your loss.

Your capacity for joy isn't diminished by loss, it's often deepened by it. You know now how precious good moments are. Don't waste them.

> TAKE STOCK
> **When was the last time you felt genuinely happy without thinking about your loss? How did that feel?**

You're ready

You've made it through. Not without scars, setbacks, and sorrows that sometimes resurface. There are times when you've rightly headed back to the Cocoon phase. Then made your way forward again. But you've made it through.

You've developed some skills along the way. You're learning what you need and how to get it.

More losses will come — different ones, with their own challenges. Whether it's a death in the family, health issues, relationship shifts, career transitions, or any other life change, you now know something you didn't before: you have what it takes. You have your Playbook. You know how to assess what you need and take action to get it.

This isn't the end of your relationship with loss. It's the beginning of a new one.

6

Testing 1-2-3

The real test of any tool isn't whether it sounds good on paper. It's whether it actually works. And life, being life, didn't wait long to provide me with opportunities to put these new tools to the test.

In the years after I'd compiled my approach to moving through change, two more big losses came my way: becoming an empty-nester and ending my corporate career.

One I could see coming from miles away, the other was a near-term decision that changed my trajectory. Both gave me the chance to apply everything I'd learned about moving from avoidance to active navigation. Here's how it went.

Round one: Empty nest

Three years before my youngest would leave for college, I was already planning for what came next.

Not just hoping it would work out. Actually planning. I'd been thinking about this for a while: when both kids left, did I really want to be rattling around in a house filled with memories of family dinners and homework battles?

So I started talking to Connor and Kendall about moving to a new house. Somewhere that suited me better. So when they both inevitably left for college, I'd have a place I actually wanted to be. We agreed to take the plunge.

There is no doubt people thought I was nuts. But I knew exactly what I needed: to be surrounded by trees. So I found a piece of land and designed a place built for solitude and peace, where I could actually feel excited about spending time alone instead of dreading the quiet. A haven to continue my move through this life change.

We call it the Treehouse. Not because it's made from scrap lumber and rusty nails with a rope ladder and secret password, but because when you're inside, the glass walls make you feel like you're floating among the branches.

This wasn't just about real estate. Thinking back to my regulators, I knew I'd need *Nature*—lots of it, all around me. I knew I'd need spaces for both *Solitude* and *Connection*—a cozy reading nook for quiet mornings, but also room for friends to gather. I was literally building my regulators into the architecture.

Connor, my eldest, left for college two weeks after we moved in, which was perfect timing to test the theory. The house worked exactly as I'd hoped. Instead of feeling sad about his empty bedroom, I felt... settled. Ready. But Kendall leaving would be different. That would be the real empty nest—just me and the trees.

As the end of her time in high school approached, I wasn't about to just white-knuckle through those first brutal weeks alone. So I made plans in and around work for what I jokingly called my 'Empty Nester World Tour', starting right after I dropped her off. When I left her behind in her New Orleans dorm room to board my plane home, I felt the familiar punch to the gut. But I also felt something else: prepared. I had a plan.

First stop: a weekend with my beloved Aunt Judy and Uncle Joe in Texas—the kind of people who'd let me cry if I needed to but would also drag me to their favorite Tex-Mex place with the best margaritas and laughter galore. Then a personal trip to Munich for an ideas conference I'd been wanting to attend. A chance to meet new friends and learn new things in a city I hadn't visited since my 21-year-old backpacking days. The last leg was a work trip to Greenland — because nothing says 'processing major life change' like watching icebergs calve into the Arctic Ocean.

The old me would have viewed this as a way to run from my emotions. The new me knew I was running toward what I needed: *Connection, Curiosity*, and enough new sights and experiences to keep my brain occupied while it adjusted to this new reality.

The 'tour' worked exactly as designed. I cried with my family in Texas, got inspired by brilliant minds in Germany, and stood slack-jawed at the raw beauty of Greenland. By the time I returned home, I was still lonely — that part was unavoidable. But I wasn't devastated. I was ready to start figuring out what suited me during this next big change.

Round two: Corporate farewell

Thirty years into my corporate career, I made a decision that shocked even me.

It wasn't like I hated my job. Actually, I loved it. Working alongside veterans, supporting servicemen and women at military bases around the world, growing a company — all of it felt meaningful. I'd learned so much about loss, and life. Plus, after all those decades of training and practice, I was good at my job. Growing revenue, mentoring people, getting things done.

But I was also getting tired. Burnt out. And with the kids launched and more space to think, I kept coming back to the same question: what if I could take what I'd been sharing inside my company about loss and moving through change, and spread the word to a bigger audience?

At the start of that year, something clicked. Maybe it was having the Treehouse as my safe landing pad. Maybe it was knowing I'd already survived bigger uncertainties than this. But I decided to take the plunge.

This wasn't like the empty-nest transition, where I had years to prepare. This was me, sitting in my office one day, realizing I couldn't keep putting off this nagging feeling that it was time for a change, time for something new. Something that would build on the writing I'd already been doing for a few years, but would mean going all-in on an entirely new career. I knew I could lean on everything I'd built in corporate America — connecting with people, speaking in front of crowds, understanding what motivated individuals and teams — but I'd be starting over in so many ways. Maybe this was my time to emerge.

Steel Town Sue would have talked herself out of it immediately. Too risky. What if I failed? What if I couldn't make it work financially?

But I caught myself before those second arrows started flying. Instead of spiraling into worst-case scenarios, I thought through what this transition would actually require. I'd need to ramp up my *Connection* regulator — I'd miss my work family terribly. And I'd need to create structure in my days without meetings and deadlines driving everything.

It was damn hard.

But instead of trying to power through the sadness or pretend it wasn't happening, I let myself feel it. I honored what I was losing while also staying open to what might come next.

The first few months were exactly as awkward as I'd expected. I didn't change my 6am alarm—some structure felt necessary even when everything else was up for grabs. I'd wake up without meetings to rush to, without emails demanding immediate responses. Some days I felt lost without the clear identity that corporate life had provided. Other days I felt giddy with freedom.

I found myself reaching for my regulators constantly. Again, *Connection* became crucial—coffee dates with former colleagues, group exercise classes, writing sessions with the editor of my blog, Leona. I cranked up *Nature* and *Movement*, taking longer walks in the woods. And I leaned hard into *Curiosity*, diving deep into books and podcasts about writing, about creativity, about anything that might help me figure out this new path.

What surprised me was how deeply I felt the loss of my work identity. For thirty years, I'd been part of corporate America. Now I was... what? Aspiring writer? Former executive? It took months to stop introducing myself by what I used to do.

But slowly, something new emerged. Not a replacement for who I'd been, but an evolution. All those skills I'd built—connecting with people, synthesizing complex information, speaking confidently—they didn't disappear. They just found new outlets. Including the book you are reading right now.

These weren't easy transitions. Both brought their own flavor of loss, their own challenges, their own moments of doubt. But what was different this time around was that I wasn't flying blind. I had tools. I expected loss and knew how to work with it rather than against it. I had a mindset of openness, possibility, and action. I had plays to customize to my unique circumstances.

The empty nest taught me the power of planning ahead —of using knowledge about myself to actively prepare for what was coming. Leaving corporate life showed me that even change you don't see coming from a mile away can be navigated with intention when you know what you need and how to get it.

Most importantly, both experiences proved that having a Playbook doesn't eliminate the hard parts. I still felt lonely. I still struggled with identity. But I also felt capable. Prepared. Like someone who could handle whatever came next.

7
The long game

Can we get better at loss?

It's a strange question. We don't usually think about loss as something to improve on, like our poker face or parallel parking skills. But here's what I've learned: while we can't control when loss shows up or what form it takes, we absolutely can get better at moving through it.

My wish is that the actionable hope mindset and playbook approach covered earlier become your immediate, in-the-moment game plan to be used loss after loss to navigate these moments of change.

But let's think about those times when we are not right in the midst of loss. When we have the capacity to hone what I call the 'Better Skills'. Six core capabilities that I've picked up through years of research, reading, and plenty of real-world practice. They work across all kinds of losses and create the infrastructure that makes you more capable before the next loss hits. More capable of helping yourself... and others.

With the 'Betters', you become someone who does loss better — not because you're special, but because you've developed the skills.

Better stories

The stories you tell yourself about your losses shape everything that comes after. This isn't about pretending your loss was no big deal or spinning fairy tales about silver linings and everything happening for a reason. This is about something much more fundamental: how you position your loss within the larger story of your life.

Psychologists Richard McNally and Adriel Boals study a concept called 'event centrality': how we frame our difficult experiences shapes everything that follows. Some let one traumatic event become the organizing principle of their entire identity. People who frame their difficult experiences as central to 'who they are' struggle more with long-term recovery than those who see those experiences as significant chapters in a larger, ongoing story.

I've come to call this 'single chapter syndrome'. When one chapter becomes the whole book, even though you've got so many other stories to tell. Yes, that chapter changed everything. Yes, there's a clear before and after line. But it doesn't have to be the only thing people know about you, or the only lens through which you see yourself.

The difference matters. When loss becomes your defining feature, everything else becomes secondary. But when it's one important chapter among many, you create space for what comes next.

This isn't denial—it's conscious narrative construction. You're not minimizing what happened. You're deciding how much real estate it gets in the story of who you are.

Changing your story doesn't change the facts. Your loss still happened. The pain was real. The impact was significant. But facts and stories are different things. The facts are what occurred. The story is how you make sense of what those facts mean for your life going forward.

Some people get so attached to their loss story that they resist updating it, holding on to "I'm someone who can't trust again" or "My best days are behind me", long after that narrative stopped serving them.

But here's what's remarkable about human beings: our stories naturally evolve over time. What feels like "the most important thing that ever happened to me" in year one shifts as you gain distance and perspective. The narrative that once felt permanent begins to feel like what it is: one chapter in a much larger story. And that evolution creates space for something remarkable — your brain's ability to naturally let go of what no longer serves you. That's not weakness, that's wisdom in action.

> TAKE STOCK
> **When you think back to your toughest losses, did how you see them change over time?**

Better forgetting

You've been taught that forgetting is failure — a sign of aging, trauma, or mental weakness. But neuroscientist Scott Small has spent years studying what memory researchers call 'adaptive forgetting', and his research reveals something remarkable: forgetting isn't a bug in the system, it's a feature. In his book, *Forgetting: The Benefits of Not Remembering*, he writes that this kind of emotional forgetting "frees us from the prisons of pain, anguish and resentments" and that "memories are continually sculpted and… Our minds store the past less like a museum of personal history than a gallery of memory art."

Your brain actively chooses what to remember and what to let fade. It's not random decay — it's precision editing.

Small's work shows that healthy forgetting serves two crucial functions after loss. First, it dulls the emotional intensity of painful memories while preserving their factual content. You remember that your divorce happened, but the crushing shame gradually loses its bite. Second, it helps you extract useful patterns from your experience while discarding the specific details that would keep you stuck.

This isn't about suppressing memories or pretending difficult things didn't happen. It's about allowing your brain to do what it's designed to do: file away the overwhelming specifics so you can access the wisdom without reliving the trauma.

Think about it: if you remembered every detail of every painful experience with perfect clarity forever, you'd be paralyzed. You'd never leave the house. What Small calls the 'memory chisel' carefully removes the emotional barbs while leaving the important lessons intact.

The people who struggle most with moving forward after loss often fight this natural process. They work overtime to preserve every detail, afraid that forgetting means betraying what they've been through. But adaptive forgetting doesn't erase your experience—it transforms it from something that controls you into something you can bear.

This is why your stories naturally evolve over time. As your brain's memory chisel does its work, the narrative that once felt so urgent and all-consuming begins to feel like just one part of your larger story. The facts remain, but their emotional stranglehold loosens.

Trust its editing process. It is precision-engineered to help you carry wisdom without carrying wounds.

TAKE STOCK

Think about a loss from several years ago. What feels different about how you remember it now compared to how it felt in the immediate aftermath?

Better noticing

When loss hits, most of us get fixated on what's gone. The empty chair. The silent phone. The paycheck that's not coming. We become experts at cataloging absence, scanning constantly for what's missing, what's broken, what's wrong.

But there's another way to direct your attention—toward what's actually there.

This isn't about forced positivity or pretending everything's fine. It's about training yourself to see the full picture instead of just the hole in the middle of it. When you can notice what exists alongside what's missing, you stay connected to reality instead of spiraling into the void.

Professor Amishi Jha's research with the military shows that people who can redirect their focus toward the present—what they can see, hear, touch, taste right now—develop significantly more resilience when facing adversity. Your brain literally gets better at finding solid ground when everything feels unstable.

That's what noticing does, it pulls you back into what's real and immediate when grief or loss threatens to sweep you away entirely.

You can practice this anywhere. Notice the temperature of your coffee cup. The weight of your feet on the ground. The colors in the sky right now. The fact that your heart is beating. The sound of traffic outside. These aren't incidental—they're anchors.

Better noticing means training your attention like you'd train any other skill. Instead of automatically scanning for problems, you deliberately look for what's working, what's present, what's still solid. The friend who did show up. The body that's still functioning. The roof over your head. The fact that you made it through yesterday.

The people who navigate loss well over time aren't naturally more optimistic. They've just gotten good at steering their attention toward what serves them instead of what takes them down. You can learn this too. Your attention is trainable, and directing it skillfully might be the most important capability you ever develop.

TAKE STOCK

Right now, without moving, what are five things you can notice with your senses? How does focusing on what's actually present change how you feel?

Better boundaries

Most people think boundaries are about saying no. But boundaries work both ways — sometimes you need to let more in, sometimes you need to keep more out.

Building healthy boundaries is one of the most valuable skills you can develop for navigating loss over time. Because loss doesn't just affect you — it affects how everyone around you relates to you. And without good boundaries, other people's discomfort with your experience can make everything harder.

If you're someone who tends to let everyone weigh in on your life — accepting unsolicited advice about how to handle your divorce, listening to friends suggest miracle cures for your health condition, or letting people minimize your struggles — you need boundaries that protect your autonomy. Your losses don't need everyone's commentary.

If you're someone who tends to shut everyone out when things get difficult — declining support, never sharing what you're going through, or refusing practical help, you need boundaries that actually allow connection. Isolation isn't protection from future loss, it's cutting yourself off from what helps you thrive.

What might good boundaries look like? Being selective about who gets to offer opinions on your life decisions. Asking for specific help when you need it without feeling obligated to accept advice you didn't request. Saying no to social obligations that drain you while staying open to meaningful connections.

The goal isn't to keep the world out or let everyone in. It's to create sustainable relationships where you can show up as yourself rather than constantly adapting to what others expect from you.

Whether your instinct is to shut everyone out or let everyone in, you can learn to create boundaries that actually serve you. It's a skill and, like any skill, you can get better at it. The payoff isn't just surviving loss better — it's having relationships that actually add to your life instead of draining it, and having energy left over for what you actually care about.

TAKE STOCK

Are you someone who lets everyone weigh in on your life, or someone who shuts people out when things get tough? What would better boundaries look like for you?

Better acceptance

The people who handle loss well over time have learned to work with reality instead of against it. This isn't about becoming zen or passive in the face of difficulty. It's about developing the capability to distinguish between what you can control and what you can't—and directing your energy accordingly.

Most of us learn acceptance the hard way, by repeatedly banging our heads against walls that aren't going to move. But some people develop this skill more deliberately, recognizing that resistance to reality is one of the biggest drains on the energy they need to actually move forward.

Psychologist Steven Hayes makes a crucial distinction between 'clean pain' and 'dirty pain' in his book, *Acceptance and Commitment Therapy: The Process and Practice of Mindful Change*. He writes, "Clean pain is the original discomfort we feel in response to a real-life problem. Dirty pain is the pain we get when we needlessly struggle to control, eliminate, or avoid clean pain." In other words, clean pain is the unavoidable hurt that comes with loss. Dirty pain is all the extra suffering we create by fighting what's already happened—the mental loops of "this shouldn't have happened", the energy spent wishing things were different, the resentment that this happened to us instead of someone else. As he says, "Contend with clean pain. Avoid dirty pain."

People who get 'better' at loss learn to recognize when they're creating dirty pain and redirect that energy toward what they can actually influence. Not because they're Zen masters, but because they've gotten good at catching themselves mid-tantrum against reality.

This capability becomes invaluable across your lifetime. Health diagnoses, career setbacks, relationship endings, family changes — the ability to work with what is rather than waste energy fighting what can't be changed becomes one of your most reliable tools for moving through any unwanted change.

Better acceptance doesn't mean you become a doormat or stop advocating for yourself. It means you get clearer about where your power actually lies. You stop exhausting yourself trying to change the unchangeable and focus your energy on the things you can actually influence. It turns you into someone who doesn't waste time fighting facts — you see what's real and get busy working with it. That kind of clarity serves you well.

> TAKE STOCK
> **When faced with things outside your control, what's your natural response? What have you learned about when to keep pushing versus when to redirect your energy?**

Better consoling

All these Better Skills matter, and they'll serve you well. But here's the lesson that took me forever to learn: you can't do loss alone.

No matter how good you get at navigating change, moving through loss is a team sport. We all take turns being the person who needs help and the person who provides it. And here's the thing: most people avoid other people's pain not because they don't care, but because they don't know what to do.

They're scared of saying the wrong thing, making it worse, or facing their own mortality. So they craft elaborate excuses and vanish precisely when their support matters most.

But consoling isn't rocket science. And you're already more capable than you think.

I feel as strongly about this as I do about learning to navigate loss itself. We can absolutely get better at consoling.

I've been consoled well through all my losses, and it made all the difference. When I was deep in grief, Takis said, "Go ahead and cry. I'm right here." My work friend Mike always stayed by my side during awkward conversations when "I'm a widow" came up and others fled. After my corporate farewell, my gym partner Kavon gave me exactly what I needed — adult conversation while swinging kettlebells and talking brain science.

None of these people had special training or perfect words. They just decided that showing up mattered more than having all the answers.

Here's what we need to get straight about supporting people through loss: instead of believing some people are just 'good at handling loss' while others aren't, we need to recognize that everyone has this capacity — they just might need different supports to access it. Instead of focusing on what's wrong with someone, we should think through what conditions would help their natural ability to flourish. Instead of comparing how quickly people 'bounce back', we should honor each person's unique journey through difficulty.

These shifts aren't just semantic. They change how we approach others during life's toughest moments.

Your job isn't to fix anyone

Your job is to create conditions that support their natural healing process. Sometimes that means practical help — handling paperwork or picking up groceries. Sometimes it means emotional support — listening without trying to solve. Sometimes it means just ensuring they don't face their pain alone.

I realise it's easier said than done, but the key is figuring out what you're good at offering and what they actually need right now, then focusing on that intersection.

You don't need to be their superhero. You need to offer the specific kind of help that works for both of you.

What actually works?

Showing up imperfectly is better than than not showing up at all. Awkward words beat silence. Small, consistent actions beat grand gestures. Follow their lead on whether they want to talk about their loss or need normal conversation. And stick around when everyone else has moved on. In the weeks, months, and years after a loss, keep checking in. Keep showing up.

When you don't know what to say, admit that: "I don't know what to say, but I'm thinking of you." Don't tiptoe around their reality — name it. Name the person they lost. Name what they've been through and how strong they are. Your willingness to acknowledge what happened will help them feel less invisible.

Here's what doesn't help

Trying to fix their emotions. Comparing their loss to others. Treating them like they're fragile when they want to be included in normal life. Disappearing because it feels awkward. You can handle discomfort better than you think.

The people who console well aren't naturally gifted. They just decided that showing up for others mattered more than their own comfort. You already have what you need: your presence, your humanity, your willingness to be with someone when things get messy, the fact that you care.

That's enough. That's everything.

> TAKE STOCK
>
> **When you think about your own consoling style, what do you naturally offer — practical help, emotional support, or just steady presence? How could you lean into that strength?**

Conclusion

We've been on quite a journey together. I appreciate having you by my side. I dredged up quite a few memories while writing this book. I shed quite a few tears.

And in the process, I've become even more convinced that moving through my losses—leaning on the actionable hope mindset and my playbook tools to right my own ship—has given me a more vibrant life. Loss gave it to me.

Things are a different kind of great, just like Wayne said they would be way back in 2016. I miss Mike. But my life is gigantic, resonant, rich. My life is great. The veil of the ordinary is lifted for me, just like Bruce Springsteen observed, and it has stayed lifted. I revel in details large and small. I take it all in. I know what it is to be truly alive. My Lone Ranger days are long over, and the connections I have with other humans—from strangers to those I love deeply—are the fuel that drives my life.

This is it. This is deep, dense, vibrant living.

Loss gave it to me. Because:

- **I shifted my mindset.** I opened to possibility. I believed in my capacity to heal. I engaged in every possible way in my path forward.

- **I built my Playbook**, and have chosen, customized, and added plays as I've moved through my various losses.
- **I've gotten so much better at moving through change,** especially in telling better stories, and my noticing skills are next level.
- **I know how to console.** I apply that knowledge, early and often.

I have one last story to leave you with.

It involves a letter. A letter written by Mike a decade before he died.

About a year after Mike's death, I was digging through a box of letters, sticky notes, scrap paper, and cards. I'd gathered up all the written evidence of his love for us and looked through it often to feel closer to him. But on this particular evening, I found something I hadn't seen before. Mike's beautiful handwriting on a lined notebook page. I pulled it out and began reading.

Dear Sweetheart...

In the letter, he talks about how Connor, Kendall, and I had changed his life. How we helped him piece his life back together after the loss of his mom. How much joy we bring him. Then, this:

> *Sometimes when I fly, I think about what would happen if you, Connor and Kendall were without me. Would you be ok? Have I done enough? Maybe it's just the good old provider instinct in me.*
>
> *But if something should happen, please know that what I want for you and for the rest of my family is to live your lives fully and happily.*

Fully and happily

I wrote this book because that's the life I want for you, too. A life lived fully and happily. Despite our losses. Not just as an instruction or directive, but as a wish born from love and faith in who we are and what we are capable of when we purposefully move through change.

Change your mindset. Develop your Playbook. Hone your skills for the long haul. Navigate your losses with knowledge and action and you will have a vibrant, rich, deep life too. You will live fully and happily.

Because that's what Mike Deagle is telling all of us to do.

And that's my sincere hope and wish for you too.

Resources

Simple words in a search bar will get you to podcasts, newsletters, blogs, books, articles, and human beings who can assist in building your path through change. Below are the resources that made the biggest impact on my thinking.

Favorite memoirs

A Grief Observed by C.S. Lewis
You have far more in common with a 1950s Oxford don who conjured up Narnia than you think.

The Year of Magical Thinking by Joan Didion
Lean prose that illuminates what's actually happening in our minds during loss.

The Light of the World by Elizabeth Alexander
Lyrical, lovely, poetic.

Making Toast by Roger Rosenblatt
A writer's description of the early months after losing his adult daughter.

Lost & Found by Kathryn Schulz
A brilliant sharing of the both/and of loss.

Rockstar memoirs

They live lives bigger than us mere mortals, and loss is threaded throughout.

Faith, Hope and Carnage by Nick Cave
Born to Run by Bruce Springsteen
The Storyteller by Dave Grohl
Broken Horses by Brandi Carlile
Greenlights by Matthew McConaughey

Storytelling

These books share the insights of people working their way through change in the most relatable way: stories.

Kitchen Table Wisdom by Rachel Naomi Remen
The Rise by Sarah Lewis
Living with our Dead by Delphine Horvilleur
Bittersweet by Susan Cain

Volumes on encouragement

Keep Moving by Maggie Smith
The Comfort Book by Matt Haig
What If It All Goes Right? by Scarlet Keys

Science

The Other Side of Sadness and *The End of Trauma* by George A. Bonanno
Ordinary Magic by Ann S. Masten
Forgetting by Scott A. Small
A Liberated Mind by Steven C. Hayes
Before and After Loss by Lisa M. Shulman

And sometimes only a poet will do

Consolations: The Power of Everyday Words by David Whyte
Upstream by Mary Oliver
The Poetry Pharmacy edited by William Sieghart
The Art of Losing edited by Kevin Young

Nothing beats speaking to a trained therapist, so please do seek professional help and support if you need to.

Connor, Kendall & Sue

Connor, Mike & Kendall

About the author

Sue Deagle is a writer, speaker, and storyteller. She is a proud product of Pennsylvania steel country and a three-decade veteran of corporate America. The best job she ever had was working around the globe with veterans and active duty military who taught her life-changing lessons about resilience and community.

Sue writes and speaks internationally on the art of thriving amid uncertainty, the power of everyday wonder, and how to trust our own capacity for change when life demands it. Her story has been featured in the *Wall Street Journal*, and she blogs weekly on her Substack, *The Luminist*.

Insatiably curious, Sue has walked 500 kilometers across Scandinavia and studied everything from mindfulness to memory.

When she's not on the move, you can find Sue at home in Virginia in her modern-day treehouse planning her next adventure, hiking along the Potomac River, lost in a good book, or laughing with her friends.

She's the mother of Connor and Kendall, who delight her with their wit, challenge her with their ideas, and help her to live a life that's a different kind of great.

suedeagle.com | *theluminist.substack.com*

Thanks

A heartfelt thanks to all those who have shaped my life, and by extension, this book.

My family, thank you for always being there. Always.

My friends, thank you for the unique gifts each of you have shared with me, and your steadfast support.

My work family, thank you for all the conversations, for astounding me with the amazing things you do to serve our soldiers, sailors, and airmen, and for giving me the chance to learn from our military and from you. What a profound gift you gave me, just when I needed it.

Leona, thank you for materializing on that Telluride trail, for being the best creative partner ever, and for becoming a friend of my heart. This book does not exist without you.

David, Clare, Lia, and everyone at the Do Lectures for giving me a community and way to contribute.

James, thank you for a gorgeous cover that says it all.

Miranda and Jess at Do Books, thank you for sharing my deep commitment to this subject, for your endless patience, and for your guidance in making these pages sing.

Connor and Kendall, thank you for your love and wit and laughter. Becoming your mom is the best thing that ever happened to me.

And Mike, thank you for all of it...

Books in the series

Do Agile Tim Drake
Do Beekeeping Orren Fox
Do Birth Caroline Flint
Do Bitcoin Angelo Morgan-Somers
Do Breathe Michael Townsend Williams
Do Build Alan Moore
Do Conversation Robert Poynton
Do Deal Richard Hoare & Andrew Gummer
Do Death Amanda Blainey
Do Design Alan Moore
Do Disrupt Mark Shayler
Do Drama Lucy Gannon
Do Earth Tam Omond
Do Ferment Matthew Pennington & Nicola Cradock
Do Fly Gavin Strange
Do Grow Alice Holden
Do Hope Gail Muller
Do Improvise Robert Poynton
Do Inhabit Sue Fan & Danielle Quigley
Do Interesting Russell Davies
Do Lead Les McKeown
Do Listen Bobette Buster
Do Loss Sue Deagle
Do Maintain Gareth Heaton
Do Make James Otter
Do Nourish Sarah Bayliss
Do Open David Hieatt
Do Pause Robert Poynton
Do Photo Andrew Paynter
Do Present Mark Shayler
Do Preserve Anja Dunk, Jen Goss & Mimi Beaven
Do Protect Johnathan Rees
Do Purpose David Hieatt
Do Recruit Khalilah Olokunola
Do Reset Jillian Lavender
Do Scale Les McKeown
Do Sea Salt Alison, David & Jess Lea-Wilson
Do Sing James Sills
Do Smoke Jen Goss & Scott Davis
Do Sourdough Andrew Whitley
Do Start Dan Kieran
Do Story Bobette Buster
Do Team Charlie Gladstone
Do Walk Libby DeLana
Do Wild Baking Tom Herbert

Also available

The Book of Do ed. Miranda West
Path Louisa Thomsen Brits
The Skimming Stone Dominic Wilcox
Stay Curious Clare Hieatt
The Path of a Doer David Hieatt

Available in print, digital and audio formats from booksellers or via our website: **thedobook.co**. To hear about events and forthcoming titles, find us on social media **@dobookco**, or subscribe to our newsletter.